FOLLOW THE HEN PATH TO ENLIGHTENMENT.

ARIEL BOOKS

**Andrews McMeel
Publishing**

Kansas City

# HARRIET
## THE ZEN HEN

DEBBIE KELLER

DESIGNED BY DIANE HOBBING

PHOTOS COURTESY OF MARJORIE HOFFMANN,
PICTUREQUEST, PHOTODISC, CREATUS, DIGITAL VISION,
AND PHOTOS.COM

06 07 08 09 10 TWP 10 9 8 7 6 5 4 3 2 1

ISBN-13: 978-0-7407-5728-0
ISBN-10: 0-7407-5728-8

LIBRARY OF CONGRESS CONTROL NUMBER:
2005929784

WWW.ANDREWSMCMEEL.COM

WE ARE WHAT WE THINK WE ARE. HEN OR CHICKEN, THE CHOICE IS YOURS.

(HARRIET)

FIRST THERE IS A FEED BUCKET.
THEN THERE IS NO FEED BUCKET.
THEN THERE IS.

IF A MAN LIVES A PURE LIFE,
NOTHING CAN DESTROY HIM.
IF A HEN LIVES A PURE LIFE,
SHE CAN BE CERTIFIED 100 PERCENT ORGANIC.

# THE WISE FARMER

TWO ZEN HENS WERE INVITED TO A FARMER'S HOUSE FOR A TEA CEREMONY. UPON ARRIVING, ONE HEN SAID TO THE FARMER, "YOU ARE WISE AND HAVE THE ABILITY TO LEARN ZEN."

THE OTHER HEN TURNED TO HER. "FOOL!" SHE CACKLED. "WHY DO YOU FLATTER THE FARMER? HE MAY ACT WISE, BUT IT IS ONLY A TRICK TO BAKE US IN A POT PIE."

SO THE FARMER BAKED THE SECOND HEN AND STUDIED ZEN WITH THE FIRST.

NEITHER FIRE NOR WIND,
BIRTH NOR DEATH, CAN TELL US
WHICH CAME FIRST.

JOY FOLLOWS PURITY OF THOUGHT LIKE A SHADOW
THAT NEVER LEAVES. IT ALSO FOLLOWS THE FEED BUCKET.

SUN SETS, GRILL IS LIT
RED BLOOD
BUT WHITE MEAT

LET US RISE UP AND BE THANKFUL!

IF WE DIDN'T LEARN A LOT TODAY,
AT LEAST WE LEARNED A LITTLE!

AND

IF WE DIDN'T LEARN A LITTLE,
AT LEAST WE DIDN'T GET SICK!
AND IF WE GOT SICK, AT LEAST WE
WEREN'T PLUCKED NAKED AND
SERVED ON A PLATTER WITH
ROASTED POTATOES!

SO, LET US BE THANKFUL!

# ONLY THE BEST

WHEN SCRATCHING AROUND THE BARNYARD ONE DAY, A
HEN OVERHEARD A CONVERSATION BETWEEN THE FARMER
AND HIS CUSTOMER.

"GIVE ME YOUR BEST FRYER," SAID THE CUSTOMER.

"EVERYTHING ON MY FARM IS THE BEST," REPLIED THE
FARMER. "YOU CANNOT FIND HERE ANY CHICKEN THAT IS
NOT THE BEST."

AT THESE WORDS THE HEN BECAME ENLIGHTENED.

THREE THINGS CANNOT BE LONG HIDDEN: THE SUN, THE MOON, AND THE BIN IN WHICH THE FARMER STORES HIS FEED.

THE TIGHTER YOU SQUEEZE, THE SMALLER THE OMELET.

# TIME TO MEDITATE

IT WAS THE RITUAL IN ANCIENT CHINA FOR THE HENS TO
MEDITATE EVERY AFTERNOON AT PRECISELY ONE O'CLOCK.

ONE SULTRY SUMMER AFTERNOON, TWO HENS WENT INTO
THEIR COOP TO MEDITATE AS USUAL, SHUTTING THE DOOR
BEHIND THEM. THE AIR WAS SO WARM AND THICK ONE HEN
FELL ASLEEP. SHE AWOKE, ALONE, THREE HOURS LATER TO
THE SMELL OF CHICKEN SOUP.

"I SHOULD HAVE REALIZED, I SHOULD HAVE REALIZED," SHE
CRIED TO HER FRIEND, AS IF SHE WERE STILL BESIDE HER.
SINCE THEN, HENS MEDITATE IN SECRET.

ENLIGHTENED HENS
KNOW SALMONELLA
IS THE SWEETEST REVENGE

SITTING QUIETLY, DOING NOTHING, SPRING COMES, THE GRASS GROWS, AND YOUR CHILDREN ARE HARD-BOILED AND DYED.

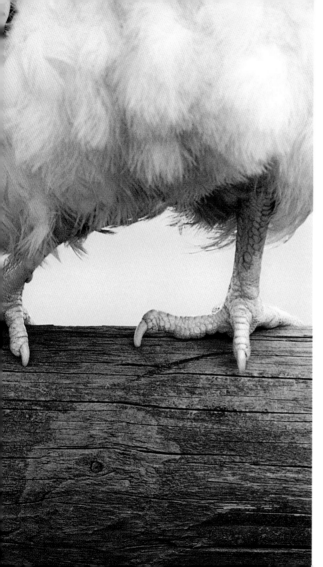

THE FOOT FEELS THE PERCH
WHEN IT FEELS THE PERCH.

A DOG IS NOT CONSIDERED A GOOD DOG BECAUSE HE IS A GOOD BARKER. A MAN IS NOT CONSIDERED A GOOD MAN BECAUSE HE IS A GOOD LISTENER. BUT A HEN MAY BE CONSIDERED A GOOD HEN IF SHE IS A GOOD LAY.

# EARTHWORMS

SEEKING ENLIGHTENMENT, A CHICK ASKED HER MASTER, "BEFORE THE EARTHWORM HAS EMERGED FROM THE GROUND, WHAT IS IT?"

HER MASTER SAID, "AN EARTHWORM."

THE CHICK PURSUED. "AFTER THE EARTHWORM HAS EMERGED FROM THE GROUND, WHAT IS IT?"

HER MASTER REPLIED, "BREAKFAST."

AS A ROOSTER WAKES
HIS FARM, AS A HEN
LAYS HER EGGS, AS A
COW GIVES HER MILK,
THE WISE PROLONG
THEIR LIVES.

WHAT YOU ARE IS WHAT YOU HAVE BEEN, AND WHAT YOU WILL BE IS A NUGGET IN A KID'S MEAL.

DO NOT DWELL IN THE PAST, DO NOT DREAM OF THE FUTURE; CONCENTRATE THE MIND ON THE PRESENT MOMENT, ESPECIALLY IF EARTHWORMS ARE NEAR.

BETTER THAN A THOUSAND HOLLOW WORDS IS ONE WORD THAT BRINGS PEACE: "DINNER!"

# SCRAMBLED EGGS

A NESTING HEN, WANTING TO IMPRESS HER ZEN MASTER, SAID, "THERE IS ONLY NOTHING. THE NATURE OF PHENOMENA IS EMPTINESS. THERE IS NOTHING TO GIVE AND NOTHING TO BE RECEIVED. THERE IS NO THING—NO SORROW, NO WISDOM, NO REALIZATION, NO DISAPPOINTMENT."

THE MASTER SAT STILL AND SAID NOTHING. SUDDENLY, HE PUSHED THE HEN OFF HER NEST AND STOLE THE EGGS SHE HAD JUST LAID. THIS MADE THE YOUNG HEN ANGRY.

"GIVE ME BACK MY EGGS!" SHE CRIED.

"WHAT EGGS?" INQUIRED THE MASTER.

IT IS BETTER TO TRAVEL
WELL THAN TO ARRIVE,
EXCEPT WHEN YOU'RE
THE ONLY COCK IN THE
HENHOUSE.

A GENEROUS HEART, KIND SPEECH, AND A LIFE OF SERVICE AND COMPASSION MIGHT RENEW YOUR HUMANITY, BUT YOU WILL STILL NEVER FLY.

TO BE PRODUCTIVE IS A HEN'S WAY OF LIFE,

TO BE IDLE IS TO LIVE THE LIFE OF A CHICKEN,

AND TO FAIL AT BOTH IS TO BE A TURKEY.

# OUTSIDE IN

ONE DAY A ZEN HEN STOOD OUTSIDE THE SLAUGHTERHOUSE DOOR.

THE FARMER CALLED TO HER, "CHICKEN, CHICKEN, WHY DO YOU NOT ENTER?"

THE HEN REPLIED, "I DO NOT SEE MYSELF AS OUTSIDE. WHY ENTER?"

LIKE EVIL AND GOOD,
THERE HAVE TO BE
ROOSTERS SO THAT
HENS CAN PROVE
THEIR PURITY ABOVE
THEM.

THERE IS NO FIRE LIKE PASSION, NO SHARK LIKE HATRED, NO SNARE LIKE FOLLY, NO FLOOD LIKE THAT WHICH MAY BE SEEN AFTER THE FARMER LEAVES THE HENHOUSE DOOR AJAR.

# THE MOST VALUABLE THING
# IN THE WORLD

ONE DAY A YOUNG CHICK, SCRATCHING IN THE GARDEN,
ASKED HER ZEN MASTER, "WHAT IS THE MOST VALUABLE
THING IN THE WORLD?"

THE MASTER REPLIED, "YOU'RE STANDING ON IT."

"OF COURSE! THE EARTH!" SAID THE CHICK.

"NO, IDIOT. SNAIL SLIME," SAID THE MASTER. "BECAUSE NO
ONE CAN NAME ITS PRICE."

SHE WHO
ENVIES
OTHERS DOES
NOT OBTAIN
PEACE OF MIND,
BUT MAY END
UP WITH THE
BEST DECORATED
ROOST IN THE
HENHOUSE.

BLIND ROOSTER CROWS
AT MIDNIGHT
ANGRY HENS, NO QUICHE TODAY

THE OBSTACLE IS THE PATH TO THE SLAUGHTERHOUSE.

HAPPINESS DECREASES BY BEING SHARED.
DOZENS OF KABOBS CAN BE MADE FROM A SINGLE
RHODE ISLAND RED.

## CROSSING THE ROAD

TWO HENS TRAVELING DOWN A MUDDY PATH CAME TO A HANDSOME ROOSTER PONDERING THE ROAD.

"A PENNY FOR YOUR THOUGHTS," SAID THE YOUNGER HEN.

"I'M AFRAID TO CROSS IT," SAID THE ROOSTER.

THE YOUNG HEN LIFTED THE ROOSTER IN HER WINGS AND CARRIED HIM TO THE OTHER SIDE.

THAT NIGHT IN THE HENHOUSE, THE OLDER HEN SAID, "WE HENS DON'T GO NEAR ROOSTERS, ESPECIALLY HANDSOME ONES. IT IS DANGEROUS FOR OUR UNFERTILIZED EGGS."

"I LEFT THE BOY THERE," SAID THE YOUNG HEN. "WHY ARE YOU STILL CARRYING HIM?"

BEFORE ENLIGHTENMENT I PECKED FEED AND LAID EGGS;

AFTER ENLIGHTENMENT I PECKED FEED AND LAID EGGS.

BOOK DESIGN AND COMPOSITION BY DIANE HOBBING OF SNAP-HAUS GRAPHICS IN DUMONT, N.J.